The Score-Raising Vocabulary Builder for GRE, GMAT, LSAT and MCAT Study

Level 1

Paul G Simpson IV

with

the Staff of Test Professors

© Copyright 2012 by Fusion Press

All rights reserved.

No part of this book may be reproduced in any form by photostat, microfilm, xerography, or any other means, or incorporated into any information retrieval system, electronic or mechanical, without the written permission of the copyright owner.

All inquiries should be addressed to:
www.testprofessors.com

Printed in the United States of America

* GRE, GMAT, LSAT, and MCAT are registered trademarks. None of their rights holders were involved in the production of, or endorse, this book.

ISBN 978-1-937599-17-1

Acknowledgments

Special thanks to David Hao for his recommendations and suggestions.

The Score-Raising Vocabulary Builder for GRE, GMAT, LSAT and MCAT Study

Level 1

Table of Contents

Level A Vocabulary — 9

    Rapid Review 1 — 16
    Rapid Review 2 — 23
    Rapid Review 3 — 30
    Level A Review — 37

Level B Vocabulary — 43

    Rapid Review 5 — 50
    Rapid Review 6 — 57
    Rapid Review 7 — 64
    Level B Review — 71

Level C Vocabulary — 77

    Rapid Review 9 — 84
    Rapid Review 10 — 91
    Rapid Review 11 — 98
    Level C Review — 105

Answer Keys — 111

Quick Lists — 119

LEVEL A VOCABULARY

EXPLAIN

Clarify (verb)

Because he had not studied the proposed bill in depth, he was unable to clarify its details to the reporters who pressed him for answers.

Other Common Forms: clarification (noun)

Delineate (verb)

She worked on the annotated version of the novel, cramming it with footnotes, until she felt it could not be delineated any further.

Other Common Forms: delineation (noun)

Elucidate (verb)

The culinary instructor elucidated the proper procedure for roasting lamb until all the steps were lucid in the students' minds.

Other Common Forms: elucidation (noun)

ARGUE FOR

Affirm (verb)

The circuit court <u>affirmed</u> the correctness of the initial judgment in a unanimous decision.

>*Other Common Forms: affirmation (noun)*

Contend (verb)

The professor's <u>contention</u> that the invasion of Normandy played no positive role in the Allies' victory in World War II was hotly disputed in her field.

>*Other Common Forms: contention (noun)*
>
>>*contentious (adjective)*

Justify (verb)

Caught up in a scandal of extortion and bribery, the congressman quickly decided to resign rather than to attempt to <u>justify</u> his actions.

>*Other Common Forms: justification (noun)*

ARGUE AGAINST

Dispel (verb)   *eliminate*

Speculation regarding her death reached such a frenzy that the actress was forced to appear on live television in order to dispel it.

Dispute (verb, noun)

After he discovered several strange purchases on his monthly statement, Juan called the credit card company to dispute them.

Other Common Forms: disputant (noun ⚓)

Rebut (verb)

The jury found the rebuttals of the defense attorney so effective that they found the defendant not guilty in less than one hour.

Other Common Forms: rebuttal (noun)

Refute (verb)

Opponents of the bill refuted its purported benefits in such devastating detail that its sponsor immediately acknowledged defeat by quickly canceling the scheduled vote.

Other Common Forms: refutation (noun)

EMPHASIZE

Stress (verb, noun)

He stressed his commitment to the afterschool program by declining to draw a salary so that it could remain open in the face of large budget cuts.

Underscore (verb)

The newspaper underscored the magnitude of the disaster by devoting its entire first section to coverage of it.

CONFUSED

Bedeviled (adjective)

The math problem bedeviled him so much that he could not even start it, though he had already spent eight hours trying to do so.

Other Common Forms: bedevil (verb)

Dumbfounded (adjective)

The variety of perfumes at the department store dumbfounded her, leaving her paralyzed and unable to make any decisions among them.

Other Common Forms: dumbfound (verb)

Quizzical (adjective)

Human expressions of quizzicality are not unique, as chimpanzees also utilize raised eyebrows and open mouths to signify confusion.

Other Common Forms: quizzicality (noun)

RAPID REVIEW #1

Find the synonym.

1) Affirm
    (A) delineate
    (B) dispute
    (C) justify
    (D) underscore

2) Dispel
    (A) contend
    (B) underscore
    (C) dumbfound
    (D) rebut

3) Elucidation
    (A) quizzicality
    (B) clarification
    (C) contention
    (D) disputant

4) Bedevil
    (A) dumbfound
    (B) stress
    (C) justify
    (D) dispel

Level A Vocabulary

5) Dispute

   (A) bedevil

   (B) affirm

   (C) delineate

   (D) refute

6) Stress

   (A) dumbfound

   (B) underscore

   (C) justify

   (D) refute

7) Quizzicality

   (A) affirmation

   (B) refutation

   (C) delineation

   (D) bedevilment

8) Rebut

   (A) dispute

   (B) contend

   (C) elucidate

   (D) underscore

MOCK

Spoof (verb, noun)

Every year at the National Correspondents Dinner, comedians are invited to <u>spoof</u> the president and the political culture of Washington.

Taunt (verb, noun)

In online role-playing games, the job of tank players is to <u>taunt</u> enemies so that they can absorb the brunt of the ensuing damage and thereby protect their weaker teammates.

QUESTIONING / DOUBTFUL

Cynical (adjective)

Jefferson argued that a <u>cynical</u> public, filled with those who question public officials, is vital to a healthy democracy.

Other Common Forms: cynicism (noun)

cynic (noun ⚥)

Evaluative (adjective)

The foundation of empirical science rests upon a set of <u>evaluative</u> measures meant to ensure thorough investigation of phenomena.

Other Common Forms: evaluation (noun)

evaluate (verb)

INDIFFERENT / LAZY

Dispirited (adjective)

After he had been fired from the job that he had held for 20 years, Peter was so dispirited that he rarely left his bed for six months.

Other Common Forms: dispirit (verb)

Idle (adjective)

The player was rebuked by her coach because she remained idle on the bench rather than engaged in the game her teammates were playing.

Other Common Forms: idleness (noun)

Slothful (adjective)

After he was diagnosed with chronic fatigue syndrome, his teachers realized that his slothfulness was not due to a lack of willpower but rather due to a serious medical condition.

Other Common Forms: slothfulness (noun)

PASSIONATE

Zeal (noun)

On June 21ˢᵗ of each year, skateboarding <u>zealots</u> gather together to hold competitions and skate through the streets.

Other Common Forms: zealous (adjective)
zealot (noun ⚓)

Zest (noun)

The <u>zest</u> with which she cooked translated well on television, where her passion captivated millions of viewers across the nation.

Other Common Forms: zestful (adjective)

PRAISE

Eulogy (noun)

In the Gettysburg Address, Abraham Lincoln delivered the greatest eulogy ever bestowed upon the fallen soldiers of the Civil War.

Other Common Forms: eulogize (verb)

Exalt (verb)

Of all the great poets in the English language, Shakespeare remains among the most exalted.

Other Common Forms: exaltation (noun)

Hail (verb)

Though it was widely ignored upon its release in 1941, *Citizen Kane* is now widely hailed as the best American film of all time.

Kudos (noun)

After the account executive won the large corporate account, which was worth millions to the agency, she received kudos from the entire office.

RAPID REVIEW #2

Find the synonym.

1) Idle
   (A) zealous
   (B) cynical
   (C) zestful
   (D) slothful

2) Kudos
   (A) cynicism
   (B) eulogy
   (C) zeal
   (D) evaluation

3) Hail
   (A) spoof
   (B) dispirit
   (C) exalt
   (D) evaluate

4) Spoof
   (A) dispirit
   (B) taunt
   (C) exalt
   (D) hail

Level A Vocabulary   www.testprofessors.com

5) Dispirited

   (A) zestful

   (B) cynical

   (C) zealous

   (D) idle

6) Cynical

   (A) evaluative

   (B) slothful

   (C) zestful

   (D) idle

7) Zeal

   (A) evaluation

   (B) exaltation

   (C) kudos

   (D) zest

8) Eulogize

   (A) taunt

   (B) hail

   (C) spoof

   (D) dispirit

CRITICIZE / SCOLD

Chasten (verb)

Upon turning in the last in a series of incomplete and sloppy assignments, Sean was <u>chastened</u> by his irate professor.

Chastise (verb)

Brandy felt <u>chastised</u> by the work ethic of all the other players, and she immediately doubled her practice time in order to contribute more to the team.

Other Common Forms: chastisement (noun)

Rebuke (verb, noun)

In a final <u>rebuke</u>, the senator left the Republican party and became an Independent member of congress.

Reprove (verb)

Angelina repeatedly <u>reproved</u> the young puppy, in a firm and timely manner, until he learned to become house-broken.

DISLIKE / HATE

Abominate (verb)

Critics of the nuclear bombings of Hiroshima and Nagasaki condemned the acts as true <u>abominations</u> that deserved only the highest censure.

Other Common Forms: abomination (noun)

Contempt (noun)

Assault and robbery are always wrong, but the mugging of the elderly, particularly those who are disabled, is beyond <u>contemptible</u>.

Other Common Forms: contemptible (adjective)

Loathe (verb)

Upon receiving a diagnosis of dyslexia, Tim finally understood the reason that he had always <u>loathed</u> reading-intensive courses so much.

Other Common Forms: loathsome (adjective)

FLATTER

Bootlick (verb)

Fearful of the competence of her colleagues, Abby resorted to bootlicking her superiors in order to ensure her job security.

Other Common Forms: bootlicker (noun ☧)

Fawn (verb)

Wearied by adulatory fans and fawning hangers-on, Mike secluded himself abroad in an attempt to reorganize his life.

Other Common Forms: fawning (adjective)

Kowtow (verb)

Sheldon insists that he is superior to everyone else and that he will not kowtow to mediocre minds.

INSULT

Affront (verb, noun)

The lawyer for the plaintiffs, who were asking for 320 million dollars in damages, argued that the counter-offer of two million dollars was an <u>affront</u> to the suffering of her clients.

Deride (verb)

When challenged to a motorcycle race, Tony stalled his bike in nervous haste and won nothing but sour <u>derision</u> from the spectators.

Other Common Forms: derision (noun)

Slight (verb, noun)

Her refusal to attend the conference was a deliberate <u>slight</u>, meant to offend the organizers whom she disliked.

Other Common Forms: slighting (adjective)

SMART

Astute (adjective)

Her colleagues valued her ability to provide astute answers to difficult questions under very tight deadlines.

Other Common Forms: astuteness (noun)

Canny (adjective)

Carrie's canny and vivid responses during the interview provided a sharp contrast to the rote answers to which the interviewer had become accustomed.

Other Common Forms: canniness (noun)

Keen (adjective)

He breezed through his dissertation defense by providing keen and insightful answers to all of the questions posed by the committee.

Other Common Forms: keenness (noun)

RAPID REVIEW #3

Find the synonym.

1) Affront
   - (A) reprove
   - (B) fawn
   - (C) deride
   - (D) loathe

2) Bootlick
   - (A) abominate
   - (B) kowtow
   - (C) chasten
   - (D) slight

3) Astute
   - (A) canny
   - (B) contemptible
   - (C) slighting
   - (D) fawning

4) Loathe
   - (A) rebuke
   - (B) affront
   - (C) kowtow
   - (D) abominate

5) Derision
 (A) abomination
 (B) affront
 (C) rebuke
 (D) astuteness

6) Chastisement
 (A) abomination
 (B) derision
 (C) keenness
 (D) rebuke

7) Slight
 (A) bootlick
 (B) deride
 (C) loathe
 (D) chastise

8) Reprove
 (A) kowtow
 (B) affront
 (C) fawn
 (D) chasten

STUPID

Dolt (noun ⚥)

Belying their reputation for <u>doltishness</u>, turtles are quite intelligent creatures that thrive around the world.

Other Common Forms: doltishness (noun)

Dullard (noun ⚥)

Daniel cultivated the image of a <u>dullard</u> when among his old friends, for he remained uneasy about his intelligence.

Other Common Forms: dull (adjective)

Obtuse (adjective)

When confronted by the intricate complexities of theoretical physics, he felt completely <u>obtuse</u> and unable to think at all clearly.

Other Common Forms: obtuseness (noun)

BRAVE

Dauntless (adjective)

After he had saved the lives of 22 residents of the town's nursing home, the firefighter received commendations for his dauntlessness.

Other Common Forms: dauntlessness (noun)

Gallant (adjective)

The odes record and praise the gallantry of brave warriors who lived in Scandinavia thousands of years ago.

Other Common Forms: gallantry (noun)

Valorous (adjective)

Despite his public stature as a war hero, he steadfastly insists that he has done nothing particularly valorous or worthy of praise.

Other Common Forms: valor (noun)

DIFFERENT / ODD

Divergent (adjective)

When naturalists first arrived on the island, they were astounded by its divergent species, many of which were found nowhere else in the world.

Other Common Forms: divergence (noun)

Heterogeneous (adjective)

Composed of people from all around the planet, the neighborhood appeals to many due to its astonishing heterogeneity of cultures.

Other Common Forms: heterogeneity (noun)

Peculiar (adjective)

Because he always wears a full suit and tie when he left the house, Tom looks extraordinarily peculiar wearing shorts and a T-shirt.

Other Common Forms: peculiarity (noun)

WIDESPREAD / OBVIOUS

Blatant (adjective)

The blatant nature of the foul made it evident, even to the spectators sitting farthest from the court.

Conspicuous (adjective)

Though he attempts to hide it, Bob's crush on the captain of the volleyball team is conspicuous enough that the entire school knows about it.

Other Common Forms: conspicuousness (noun)

SECRET / DIFFICULT TO UNDERSTAND

Clandestine (adjective)

Some military operations are so <u>clandestine</u> that the general public does not know about them until years, or even decades, after the events occurred.

Cryptic (adjective)

The ending of the story is <u>cryptic</u> enough that scholars continue to debate and offer wildly varying interpretations of it.

Inscrutable (adjective)

String theory remains <u>inscrutable</u> to those who are not severely dedicated and willing to devote several years to the study of it.

Other Common Forms: inscrutability (noun)

LEVEL A REVIEW

Find the synonym.

1) Abominate
   - (A) deride
   - (B) exalt
   - (C) loathe
   - (D) rebuke

2) Clandestine
   - (A) slothful
   - (B) evaluative
   - (C) physical
   - (D) inscrutable

3) Affirm
   - (A) justify
   - (B) taunt
   - (C) dispel
   - (D) delineate

4) Bedeviled
   - (A) gallant
   - (B) dumbfounded
   - (C) cynical
   - (D) cryptic

5) Refute

   (A) elucidate

   (B) contend

   (C) reprove

   (D) dispel

6) Chasten

   (A) abominate

   (B) slight

   (C) chastise

   (D) justify

7) Stress

   (A) clarify

   (B) underscore

   (C) rebut

   (D) spoof

8) Dispirited

   (A) zealous

   (B) quizzical

   (C) idle

   (D) contemptible

9) Eulogy

   (A) divergence

   (B) conspicuousness

   (C) doltishness

   (D) kudos

10) Blatant

   (A) conspicuous

   (B) dull

   (C) heterogeneous

   (D) loathsome

11) Dullard

   (A) dolt

   (B) disputant

   (C) bootlicker

   (D) zealot

12) Cynical

   (A) clandestine

   (B) valorous

   (C) obtuse

   (D) evaluative

13) Astute

(A) fawning

(B) dumbfounded

(C) heterogeneous

(D) keen

14) Hail

(A) spoof

(B) exalt

(C) affront

(D) kowtow

15) Dispute

(A) abominate

(B) elucidate

(C) chasten

(D) refute

16) Bootlick

(A) slight

(B) dispirit

(C) fawn

(D) eulogize

Level A Vocabulary

17) Canny
    (A) bedeviled
    (B) contemptible
    (C) contentious
    (D) astute

18) Affront
    (A) delineation
    (B) dispute
    (C) zest
    (D) derision

19) Conspicuous
    (A) divergent
    (B) blatant
    (C) zealous
    (D) dauntless

20) Gallantry
    (A) inscrutability
    (B) idleness
    (C) valor
    (D) eulogy

LEVEL B VOCABULARY

EXPLAIN

Demystify (verb)

Due to the difficulty of the topic, it took more than three semesters' worth of course work to truly demystify it.

Other Common Forms: demystification (noun)

Expound (verb)

Though Crystal expounded the idea of inflation quite well in her paper, she received a mediocre grade due to its lack of proper citations.

Other Common Forms: exposition (noun)

ARGUE FOR

Advocate (verb, noun ⚓)

A staunch <u>advocate</u> of local agriculture, Sheila only buys fruits and vegetables that are grown within 20 miles of her home.

Corroborate (verb)

He <u>corroborated</u> the available evidence by providing a credit card receipt stamped with the time of purchase.

Other Common Forms: corroboration (noun)

Substantiate (verb)

The journal article was rescinded when its authors could not <u>substantiate</u> their claim with proper experimental data.

Other Common Forms: substantiation (noun)

ARGUE AGAINST

Confute (verb)

The defendant's claim that he never left home was <u>confuted</u> by a video that showed him buying gas at a local station.

Other Common Forms: confutation (noun)

Debunk (verb)

The discovery of multitudinous species in the deep ocean <u>debunked</u> the idea that life could not exist here.

Dissent (verb, noun)

Though the measure ultimately passed, <u>dissent</u> was measured by the thousands of votes against it.

Other Common Forms: dissenter (noun ⚓)

EMPHASIZE

Accentuate (verb)

The commencement speaker advised the graduates that they would face both sad and happy times down the road, and that the key to a truly happy life was to <u>accentuate</u> the latter.

Other Common Forms: accentuation (noun)

Punctuate (verb)

Sirens and alarms <u>punctuated</u> the urgency of the situation, which required an immediate emergency response.

Other Common Forms: punctuation (noun)

CONFUSED

Befuddled (adjective)

Jim was <u>befuddled</u> when he returned home to find his phone in the refrigerator, fish swimming in his sink, and a circus in his back yard.

Other Common Forms: befuddlement (noun)

Bemused (adjective)

She was <u>bemused</u> by all the attention received by her comment, particularly since it had been stated repeatedly by others.

Other Common Forms: bemusement (noun)

Confounded (adjective)

Organic chemistry <u>confounded</u> him, until he hired a tutor to help him understand its core concepts.

Other Common Forms: confoundedness (noun)

Vexed (adjective)

The success of the game lies in its ability to <u>vex</u> players in order to intrigue them, without confusing them so much that they no longer want to play.

Other Common Forms: vexation (noun)

vex (verb)

RAPID REVIEW #5

Find the synonym.

1) Befuddlement
   (A) substantiation
   (B) accentuation
   √ (C) vexation
   (D) confutation

2) Debunk
   (A) advocate
   √ (B) dissent
   (C) expound
   (D) vex

3) Punctuation
   (A) bemusement
   (B) substantiation
   √ (C) accentuation
   (D) confutation

4) Vex
   (A) demystify
   (B) punctuate
   √ (C) confound
   (D) corroborate

Level B Vocabulary   www.testprofessors.com

5) Demystify
    (A) substantiate
    (B) debunk
    √ (C) expound
    (D) bemuse

6) Confute
    (A) advocate
    √ (B) dissent
    (C) expound
    (D) accentuate

7) Substantiate
    √ (A) corroborate
    (B) confute
    (C) vex
    (D) punctuate

8) Confoundedness
    (A) accentuation
    √ (B) befuddlement
    (C) demystification
    (D) confutation

MOCK

Jeer (verb, noun)

After the basketball player missed his first 22 shots, the crowd jeered in mock appreciation when he finally scored a basket.

Other Common Forms: jeering (adjective)

Scoff (verb, noun)

He scoffed at the idea of turning his lifetime of work in fractal mathematics into a comic book.

Other Common Forms: scoffing (adjective)

QUESTIONING / DOUBTFUL

Appraising (adjective)

The experienced collector cast an <u>appraising</u> eye over the art works, quickly confirming their authenticity.

Other Common Forms: appraise (verb)
appraisal (noun)

Incredulous (adjective)

When she realized that the winning number matched those on her ticket, she was so <u>incredulous</u> that she confirmed that they were identical at least a dozen more times.

Other Common Forms: incredulity (noun)

INDIFFERENT / LAZY

Apathetic (adjective)

Her apathy for her intended major, which she had chosen in order to placate her parents, ultimately resulted in her placement on academic probation.

Other Common Forms: apathy (noun)

Lackadaisical (adjective)

Barry's teacher is furious about his lackadaisical attitude towards school, as he works just hard enough to pass and rarely puts any thought into the assignments.

Languorous (adjective)

The languorous summer days passed by in quick succession, ultimately leaving no lasting accomplishments in their wake.

Other Common Forms: languor (noun)

Nonchalant (adjective)

John's nonchalance about proper preparation resulted in his death during a mountain-climbing expedition that he had not trained for at all.

Other Common Forms: nonchalance (noun)

PASSIONATE

Fervent (adjective)

The <u>fervor</u> of the fans cannot be understood unless one attends a match, during which no one ever sits down or stops cheering.

Other Common Forms: fervor (noun)
fervency (noun)

Fervid (adjective)

What she believed to be temporary scribbles on a <u>fervid</u> affair are now remembered as some of the most passionate love poems ever written.

Other Common Forms: fervidness (noun)

Perfervid (adjective)

As many as two-thirds of the population are far from <u>perfervid</u> about replacing the dollar bill with a dollar coin, with most citing familiarity as the primary reason.

Other Common Forms: perfervidness (noun)

PRAISE

Accolade (noun)

So multitudinous were the <u>accolades</u> for her athletic prowess that she had to construct an extra room in order to display them all.

Approbation (noun)

Richard founded the non-profit to serve the underprivileged children in the community, and not to receive any <u>approbation</u> or awards.

Herald (verb)

The novel was <u>heralded</u> by critics, who lavished praise upon the originality of its plot and characters.

Paean (noun)

Her final poem was a <u>paean</u> to New York City, which had surprised and nurtured her throughout her long career.

RAPID REVIEW #6

Find the synonym.

1) Lackadaisical
   - (A) incredulous
   - (B) perfervid
   - (C) scoffing
   - (D) languorous

2) Paean
   - (A) nonchalance
   - (B) accolade
   - (C) fervor
   - (D) appraisal

3) Fervency
   - (A) fervidness
   - (B) apathy
   - (C) appraisal
   - (D) nonchalance

4) Jeer
   - (A) approbation
   - (B) incredulity
   - (C) scoff
   - (D) languor

Level B Vocabulary

5) Approbation
    (A) incredulity
    (B) apathy
    (C) fervidness
    (D) accolade

6) Apathetic
    (A) nonchalant
    (B) scoffing
    (C) fervent
    (D) appraising

7) Fervor
    (A) languor
    (B) jeer
    (C) perfervidness
    (D) paean

8) Incredulous
    (A) perfervid
    (B) appraising
    (C) lackadaisical
    (D) jeering

CRITICIZE / SCOLD

Berate (verb)

After he disrespected the coaching staff, the rookie player was berated by his more experienced teammates.

Other Common Forms: berating (adjective)

Castigate (verb)

Though she did not enjoy castigating her children, she occasionally did so in order to teach them proper behavior.

Other Common Forms: castigation (noun)

Chide (verb)

The principal chided the students after their prank caused substantial damage to the school's auditorium.

Other Common Forms: chiding (adjective)

DISLIKE / HATE

Abhor (verb)

Mary abhorred cockroaches, so the idea of eating one, even for a prize of ten thousand dollars, thoroughly disgusted her.

Other Common Forms: abhorrent (adjective)

Antipathy (noun)

Ever since a dog unexpectedly attacked her, she has not been able to quell her fear of and antipathy towards canines.

Disdain (verb, noun)

Though the crowd's disdain for him was palpable, evident in twisted faces and cold stares, the actor nonetheless took the stage and performed well.

Other Common Forms: disdainful (adjective)

FLATTER

Blandish (verb)

Though the restaurant was overbooked for the evening, they managed to blandish the hostess into finding them a table.

Other Common Forms: blandishment (noun)

Obsequious (adjective)

Indifferent to any form of obsequiousness, whether verbal flattery or fawning gifts, the professor always graded students based solely on the quality of their work.

Other Common Forms: obsequiousness (noun)

Sycophant (noun ⚓)

The company encountered trouble when the board was packed with sycophants, who affirmed every action of the Chief Executive Officer in order to maintain favor with him.

Other Common Forms: sycophantism (noun)

INSULT

Aspersion (noun)

Though she may have had a bad experience in Japan, she should not generalize and cast <u>aspersion</u> upon the entire nation.

Besmirch (verb)

The lawsuit alleges that the newspaper article irrevocably <u>besmirched</u> the politician's reputation, and that such libel should result in punitive damages.

Other Common Forms: besmirchment (noun)

Disparage (verb)

The manager was fired after an internal investigation found that he had a long history of making <u>disparaging</u> and sexist remarks to his employees.

Other Common Forms: disparagement (noun)

SMART

Erudite (adjective)

The extended format of the show allowed the guest to share her erudition in a relaxed fashion, resulting in a captivating and intelligent conversation.

Other Common Forms: erudition (noun)

Sagacious (adjective)

The investor perceived the value of underpriced companies before his competitors, and this sagacity enabled him to amass a fortune.

Other Common Forms: sagacity (noun)

Sage (adjective, noun ⚲)

Eric never forgot the sage advice of his grandfather, who had told him to never bite the hand that feeds him and to always be appreciative of what he has.

RAPID REVIEW #7

Find the synonym.

1) Aspersion
    (A) sage
    (B) disparagement
    (C) castigation
    (D) blandishment

2) Erudite
    (A) chiding
    (B) disdainful
    (C) berating
    (D) sage

3) Castigate
    (A) disdain
    (B) besmirch
    (C) berate
    (D) abhor

4) Antipathy
    (A) disdain
    (B) obsequiousness
    (C) aspersion
    (D) sagacity

5) Sagacious
    (A) obsequious
    (B) erudite
    (C) disdainful
    (D) abhorrent

6) Berate
    (A) abhor
    (B) blandish
    (C) chide
    (D) disparage

7) Obsequiousness
    (A) erudition
    (B) sycophantism
    (C) antipathy
    (D) castigation

8) Disparage
    (A) chide
    (B) besmirch
    (C) blandish
    (D) disdain

STUPID

Dupe (verb, noun ⚓)

Using false information and the promise of quick returns, the con man <u>duped</u> hundreds of victims out of their life's savings.

Inane (adjective)

The Internet contains all types of information: keen as well as <u>inane</u>, documented as well as undocumented.

Other Common Forms: inanity (noun)

Vapid (adjective)

She felt undeserving of the millions of dollars that she had earned for <u>vapid</u> performances, particularly when many brilliant musicians struggled mightily to make a living.

Other Common Forms: vapidity (noun)

BRAVE

Audacious (adjective)

Though the boss' remarks enraged every member of the office, only Stacy had the <u>audacity</u> to address the issue with him and to ask him to apologize.

Other Common Forms: audacity (noun)

Lionhearted (adjective)

Richard the Lionheart was called such because of his reputation as a <u>lionhearted</u> military leader during the Third Crusade.

Stalwart (adjective)

Throughout her long career, she has been a <u>stalwart</u>, determined defender of her clients and her community.

Other Common Forms: stalwartness (noun)

DIFFERENT / ODD

Aberrant (adjective)

What is <u>aberrant</u> and strange to one generation often becomes completely normal to the next.

Other Common Forms: aberration (noun)

Disparate (adjective)

The teacher was officially reprimanded not for the punishment of the two students but for the <u>disparate</u> nature of the punishments that each student received.

Other Common Forms: disparateness (noun)

disparity (noun)

WIDESPREAD / OBVIOUS

Egregious (adjective)

He had to cut his trek through the Sahara Desert short because he made the egregious mistake of not packing enough water for the trip.

Other Common Forms: egregiousness (noun)

Overt (adjective)

Researchers contend that, while overt racism is no longer a prominent part of the culture, covert racism still exerts a powerful influence.

Other Common Forms: overtness (noun)

Pervasive (adjective)

The pervasiveness of illiteracy in the county has led to calls for increased school funding, additional remedial courses, and the opening of an early literacy center.

Other Common Forms: pervasiveness (noun)

SECRET / DIFFICULT TO UNDERSTAND

Abstruse (adjective)

Though the theory itself may be <u>abstruse</u>, its practical applications are widespread and relatively simple to comprehend.

Other Common Forms: abstruseness (noun)

Esoteric (adjective)

His novels are littered with forced, <u>esoteric</u> allusions that weigh down characters' dialogue and render the plot incomprehensible.

Other Common Forms: esotericism (noun)

Furtive (adjective)

With a series of <u>furtive</u> looks, James was able to see his classmates' work and then copy her answers on his test paper.

Other Common Forms: furtiveness (noun)

LEVEL B REVIEW

Find the synonym.

1) Expound
    (A) vex
    (B) blandish
    (C) demystify
    (D) berate

2) Fervent
    (A) incredulous
    (B) perfervid
    (C) aberrant
    (D) bemused

3) Befuddled
    (A) erudite
    (B) disparate
    (C) confounded
    (D) obsequious

4) Disdain
    (A) castigate
    (B) herald
    (C) abhor
    (D) appraise

Level B Vocabulary

5) Scoff

   (A) punctuate

   (B) substantiate

   (C) jeer

   (D) debunk

6) Substantiate

   (A) corroborate

   (B) chide

   (C) demystify

   (D) abhor

7) Inane

   (A) esoteric

   (B) egregious

   (C) vapid

   (D) stalwart

8) Audacious

   (A) overt

   (B) lionhearted

   (C) berating

   (D) disparate

Level B Vocabulary

9) Accolade
    (A) nonchalance
    (B) accentuation
    (C) paean
    (D) vexation

10) Apathetic
    (A) sagacious
    (B) disdainful
    (C) vapid
    (D) lackadaisical

11) Confute
    (A) dupe
    (B) dissent
    (C) castigate
    (D) expound

12) Antipathy
    (A) bemusement   dislike
    (B) blandishment
    (C) disdain
    (D) confutation

Level B Vocabulary

13) Audacity
  (A) inanity
  (B) bemusement
  (C) stalwartness
  (D) sycophantism

14) Castigate
  (A) appraise
  (B) herald
  (C) punctuate
  (D) berate

15) Languorous
  (A) egregious
  (B) lackadaisical
  (C) furtive
  (D) audacious

16) Aspersion
  (A) vapidity
  (B) abstruseness
  (C) disparagement
  (D) sagacity

17) Debunk
  (A) advocate
  (B) demystify
  (C) besmirch
  (D) confute

18) Aberrant
  (A) pervasive
  (B) disparate
  (C) apathetic
  (D) stalwart

19) Esoteric
  (A) chiding
  (B) furtive
  (C) nonchalant
  (D) fervent

20) Overt
  (A) scoffing
  (B) incredulous
  (C) egregious
  (D) confounded

LEVEL C VOCABULARY

EXPLAIN

Expatiate (verb)

Prompted by the interviewer, the director expatiated upon the intertwining themes of his many films.

Other Common Forms: expatiation (noun)

Exposit (verb)

Because the book was heavy on exposition, it irritated those readers who expected more action.

Other Common Forms: exposition (noun)

Lucubrate (verb)

The result of her long lucubration, *An Illustrated History of Ladybugs*, totals more than 3,000 pages and includes 500 original illustrations.

Other Common Forms: lucubration (noun)

ARGUE FOR

Aver (verb)

It is more helpful for children's development, researchers <u>aver</u>, to praise them for effort rather than for intelligence.

Avow (verb)

An <u>avowed</u> pacifist, the senator shocked his constituency when he voted in favor of the declaration of war.

> *Other Common Forms: avowal (noun)*
> *avowed (adjective)*

Vindicate (verb)

The mathematician never lived to see the <u>vindication</u> of her theorem, which had gained her only mocking opposition during her lifetime.

> *Other Common Forms: vindication (noun)*

ARGUE AGAINST

Controvert (verb)

He controverted his opponent's ideas so thoroughly during the debate that there was no doubt that he had won.

Gainsay (verb)

In many cultures it is an egregious sign of disrespect to gainsay one's elders, particularly if they are older relatives.

Other Common Forms: gainsayer (noun ⚚)

Repugn (verb)

Because she could repugn neither her opponent's experience nor his ideas, she resorted to calumnious attacks on his character.

EMPHASIZE

Iterate (verb)

Most of children's language development is the result of <u>iteration</u>, which allows them to master pronunciation, new vocabulary, and grammatical structures.

Other Common Forms: iteration (noun)

Reiterate (verb)

Rather than take issue with the students' failure to understand the first time, the instructor calmly <u>reiterated</u> the ideas to give them a second chance to comprehend.

Other Common Forms: reiteration (noun)

CONFUSED

Addled (adjective)

Returning to the town after an absence of 25 years, she could not find her way around, <u>addled</u> and disoriented as she was by the unfamiliar landscape.

Other Common Forms: addle (verb)
addlement (noun)

Discombobulated (adjective)

The novice teacher found himself <u>discombobulated</u> by the incessant demands and short attention spans of the twenty four-year-olds in his classroom.

Other Common Forms: discombobulation (noun)

Flummoxed (adjective)

Never having learned it growing up, she was initially <u>flummoxed</u> by the basics of personal finance such as budgeting, bookkeeping, and credit history.

Other Common Forms: flummox (verb)

Nonplussed (adjective)

The calculus class <u>nonplussed</u> him thoroughly, until he became more comfortable with the core concepts.

Other Common Forms: nonplus (verb)

RAPID REVIEW #9

Find the synonym.

1) Discombobulation
    (A) avowal
    (B) addlement
    (C) iteration
    (D) lucubration

2) Exposition
    (A) reiteration
    (B) expatiation
    (C) vindication
    (D) gainsayer

3) Controvert
    (A) aver
    (B) flummox
    (C) vindicate
    (D) gainsay

4) Iterate
    (A) exposit
    (B) reiterate
    (C) avow
    (D) addle

Level C Vocabulary

5) Expatiate
   (A) gainsay
   (B) addle
   (C) lucubrate
   (D) reiterate

6) Repugn
   (A) flummox
   (B) controvert
   (C) iterate
   (D) exposit

7) Nonplus
   (A) addle
   (B) controvert
   (C) avow
   (D) expatiate

8) Aver
   (A) exposit
   (B) flummox
   (C) vindicate
   (D) reiterate

MOCK

Deride (verb)

When the actor publically spoke about political policy, he was widely <u>derided</u> and ridiculed in the press.

Other Common Forms: derision (noun)

Lampoon (verb, noun)

Her editorial cartoons savagely <u>lampoon</u> all the leading figures of today, making her one of Britain's most feared and respected political commentators.

Other Common Forms: lampooning (adjective)

QUESTIONING / DOUBTFUL

Dubious (adjective)

When she received an email stating that she had won the Ugandan lottery, she was so dubious of its authenticity that she immediately deleted it.

Other Common Forms: dubiousness (noun)

Dubitable (adjective)

All scientific theories are dubitable, open to revision or oblivion as new evidence arises.

Other Common Forms: dubitably (adverb)

INDIFFERENT / LAZY

Indolent (adjective)

In her mid-twenties, she began to regret the <u>indolence</u> of her teenage years because it had cost her the chance at higher education.

Other Common Forms: indolence (noun)

Insouciant (adjective)

The <u>insouciance</u> of the country's leaders became a rallying cry for the opposition, which promised to listen to and address the needs of the general public.

Other Common Forms: insouciance (noun)

Otiose (adjective)

The press charged that the city council engaged only in <u>otiose</u> debate instead of focused discourse that could improve the city's dire financial situation.

Other Common Forms: otiosity, otioseness (noun)

PASSIONATE

Ardent (adjective)

While his <u>ardent</u> verses of love never did win him the heart of his beloved, they did ensure his prominence among his country's poets.

Other Common Forms: ardency (noun)

Avid (adjective)

An <u>avid</u> fan, Terry has attended every single game played by his favorite team over the course of the past thirty years.

Other Common Forms: avidness (noun)

Torrid (adjective)

The <u>torrid</u> love between Heloise and her tutor, Abelard, survives in a series of letters that they exchanged in the 12th century.

Other Common Forms: torridness (noun)

PRAISE

Adulation (noun)

Though she was grateful that critics enjoyed her work, the actress needed no such adulation to continue her work in the theater.

Éclat (noun)

The baritone's performance that night received such éclat that opera aficionados still discuss it more than 200 years later.

Encomium (noun)

The renowned journalist declared that an obituary should not be an undeserved encomium but rather a fair assessment of a life.

Extol (verb)

Design experts extolled the chair as a revolutionary reimagining that would forever change the manner in which people sit.

Panegyrize (verb)

During the prime minister's funeral, prominent officials delivered a series of panegyrics meant to burnish her reputation as a leader.

Other Common Forms: panegyric (noun)

Plaudit (noun)

It seems that, precisely because he cared so little about the plaudits of critics, these very critics felt compelled to heap more praise upon him.

RAPID REVIEW #10

Find the synonym.

1) Dubious
    (A) ardent
    (B) lampooning
    (C) dubitable
    (D) insouciant

2) Panegyric
    (A) indolence
    (B) encomium
    (C) avidness
    (D) derision

3) Torrid
    (A) otiose
    (B) dubious
    (C) lampooning
    (D) ardent

4) Insouciant
    (A) avid
    (B) dubitable
    (C) indolent
    (D) deriding

5) Avid
   (A) indolent
   (B) ardent
   (C) dubitable
   (D) deriding

6) Éclat
   (A) otiosity
   (B) plaudit
   (C) torridness
   (D) dubiousness

7) Lampoon
   (A) panegyrize
   (B) extol
   (C) adulate
   (D) deride

8) Adulation
   (A) otioseness
   (B) ardency
   (C) encomium
   (D) lampoon

CRITICIZE / SCOLD

Animadversion (noun)

Because the business announced the policy reversal during Christmas, it passed without animadversion from opponents.

Excoriate (verb)

The magnate used his will as an opportunity to excoriate those members of his family who only cared about the money that they expected to inherit.

Other Common Forms: excoriation (noun)

Remonstrate (verb)

Exhausted by a long day's work, the mother did not possess the energy to remonstrate with her son, despite the enormity of the mess that he had made in the kitchen.

Other Common Forms: remonstration (noun)

Reprobate (verb, adjective, noun)

The novel depicts the life of the reprobate Mr. Brinks, who is exiled from his community as a misguided youth, only to be embraced by it later in life.

Other Common Forms: reprobation (noun)

Upbraid (verb)

The manager had no choice but to upbraid the new employee for repeated lateness, several missed deadlines, and dismal overall performance.

DISLIKE / HATE

Animus (noun)

The tension throughout *Othello* stems, in large part, from the play's unwillingness to reveal the source of Iago's <u>animus</u> towards the title character.

Enmity (noun)

Theirs was not a true <u>enmity</u>, but a rivalry manufactured by the sport of tennis in order to generate ratings and revenue.

Execrate (verb)

The condition of the apartment unit is <u>execrable</u>, infested as it is with mice and cockroaches and overrun as it is with mold.

Other Common Forms: execrable (adjective)

Execration (noun)

FLATTER

Inveigle (verb)

By offering the illusion of entry into an exclusive club, the con man inveigled thousands of people into investing in his fraudulent Ponzi scheme.

Other Common Forms: inveiglement (noun)

Toady (noun ⚓)

She refuted the idea that she was a mere toady, who maintained her position through flattery, by pointing to several successful projects that she had spearheaded.

Truckle (verb)

When he could no longer truckle to the unreasonable demands of his boss, he quit in search of employment that did not require flattering obedience.

Other Common Forms: truckling (adjective)

Wheedle (verb)

With obsequious words and deeds, he was able to wheedle anything he liked out of his parents.

Other Common Forms: wheedling (adjective)

INSULT

Calumny (noun)

The sheer amount of <u>calumny</u> heaped upon her by the tabloids forced the actress into an extended seclusion.

Other Common Forms: calumnious (adjective)

Contumely (noun)

Though many a <u>contumacious</u> thought passed through his mind, he had the restraint and decency not to give voice to them.

Other Common Forms: contumacious (adjective)

Obloquy (noun)

Moved by the principle of equality, Nelson Mandela risked personal harm and <u>obloquy</u> for his convictions.

Traduce (verb)

The newspaper was found guilty of libel for a series of false articles that <u>traduced</u> the prominent politician and his family.

Other Common Forms: traducement (noun)

SMART

Perspicacious (adjective)

Even his staunchest adversaries had to admit that the judge was blessed with a perspicacity that marked all of his rulings.

Other Common Forms: perspicacity (noun)

Sapient (adjective)

Though reckless in other areas, Martha exhibited a sapience in her professional life that enabled her to rise to the top of her field.

Other Common Forms: sapience (noun)

Trenchant (adjective)

The researcher voiced her disagreement in a trenchant article that is both lucid in its language and persuasive in its logic.

Other Common Forms: trenchancy (noun)

RAPID REVIEW #11

Find the synonym.

1) Contumely
    (A) excoriation
    (B) trenchancy
    (C) calumny
    (D) toady

2) Sapience
    (A) perspicacity
    (B) remonstration
    (C) obloquy
    (D) animus

3) Execration
    (A) traducement
    (B) inveiglement
    (C) enmity
    (D) animadversion

4) Upbraid
    (A) wheedle
    (B) traduce
    (C) reprobate
    (D) truckle

5) Inveigle

   (A) execrate

   (B) truckle

   (C) excoriate

   (D) upbraid

6) Animus

   (A) enmity

   (B) sapience

   (C) animadversion

   (D) calumny

7) Trenchant

   (A) execrable

   (B) perspicacious

   (C) wheedling

   (D) truckling

8) Obloquy

   (A) traducement

   (B) sapience

   (C) reprobation

   (D) inveiglement

STUPID

Fatuous (adjective)

Though critics have soundly upbraided reality shows for their fatuousness, these shows continue to proliferate because of low production costs and widespread popularity.

Other Common Forms: fatuousness (noun)

Insipid (adjective)

While endlessly fascinating to the dreamer himself, these same dreams are usually found to be insipid by others.

Other Common Forms: insipidness (noun)

Vacuous (adjective)

Once thoughtful and keen, discussion on the website has become so vacuous that he has stopped visiting the site altogether.

Other Common Forms: vacuity (noun)

BRAVE

Intrepid (adjective)

The popular legend of Davey Crockett as an <u>intrepid</u> frontiersman diverges greatly from the historical figure, whose contemporaries thought indolent and cowardly.

Other Common Forms: intrepidness (noun)

Mettlesome (adjective)

The undercover agent's <u>mettle</u> was proven when she infiltrated the drug cartel for several years, until enough evidence had been gathered to arrest dozens of its members.

Other Common Forms: mettle (noun)

Stout (adjective)

The knights of medieval Europe required squires who were <u>stout</u> and would not shrink from battle.

Other Common Forms: stoutness (noun)

Stouthearted (adjective)

Ultramarathon is a sport reserved for the <u>stouthearted</u> who are willing to run, often across rugged terrain, distances as long as 100 miles.

Other Common Forms: stoutheartedness (noun)

DIFFERENT / ODD

Anomalous (adjective)

Only with the assistance of knowledgeable amateurs were astronomers able to identify the source of the anomalous light that flashed across the sky.

Other Common Forms: anomaly (noun)

Quixotic (adjective)

His desire to sail around the world on an inflatable duck was deemed too quixotic to be successful.

Other Common Forms: quixotism (noun)

Singular (adjective)

Her impact on jazz is singular, never again to be replicated by other singers, no matter their talent or success.

Other Common Forms: singularity (noun)

WIDESPREAD / OBVIOUS

Manifest (adjective)

Though his affection for Rosita was <u>manifest</u> in his words and deeds, she never realized the attraction that was immediately evident to everyone else.

Other Common Forms: manifestation (noun)

Patent (adjective)

The congressman contended that the need for new poverty initiatives was <u>patent,</u> obvious in the increasing ranks of the poor in the country.

Other Common Forms: patently (adverb)

SECRET / DIFFICULT TO UNDERSTAND

Arcane (adjective)

Her field of mathematics is so <u>arcane</u> that only a few people in the world can understand the questions that preoccupy her.

Recondite (adjective)

The professor's aim was not to dazzle his students with <u>recondite</u> knowledge but rather to engage them in a dialogue about the implications of such knowledge.

Sub-rosa (adjective)

Fearing that any publicity would ruin the delicate negotiations, the commissioner and union president held a <u>sub-rosa</u> meeting to discuss the final form of the collective bargaining agreement.

Surreptitious (adjective)

For her, <u>surreptitiousness</u> was not a choice but a necessity, one that stemmed from her classified work at the Pentagon.

Other Common Forms: surreptitiousness (noun)

LEVEL C REVIEW

Find the synonym.

1) Stout
   (A) ardent
   (B) intrepid
   (C) fatuous
   (D) manifest

2) Wheedle
   (A) execrate
   (B) flummox
   (C) lampoon
   (D) truckle

3) Addle
   (A) exposit
   (B) nonplus   *confused*
   (C) controvert
   (D) excoriate

4) Insipid
   (A) dubious
   (B) avid
   (C) insouciant
   (D) vacuous

5) Quixotic

   (A) sub-rosa

   (B) singular

   (C) nonplussed

   (D) dubitable

6) Patent

   (A) manifest

   (B) discombobulated

   (C) perspicacious

   (D) calumnious

7) Éclat

   (A) mettle

   (B) plaudit

   (C) salience

   (D) anomaly

8) Lucubrate

   (A) extol

   (B) excoriate

   (C) expatiate

   (D) wheedle

Level C Vocabulary   www.testprofessors.com

9) Arcane

   (A) addled

   (B) deriding

   (C) otiose

   (D) recondite

10) Stout-hearted

   (A) fatuous

   (B) quixotic

   (C) mettlesome

   (D) manifest

11) Aver

   (A) remonstrate

   (B) inveigle

   (C) avow

   (D) traduce

12) Excoriate

   (A) exposit

   (B) gainsay

   (C) upbraid   scold

   (D) vindicate

13) Surreptitious

   (A) indolent

   (B) trenchant

   (C) sub-rosa

   (D) calumnious

14) Repugn

   (A) nonplus

   (B) reiterate

   (C) controvert — Argue against

   (D) deride

15) Ardent

   (A) avid

   (B) otiose

   (C) sapient

   (D) stout

16) Vacuous — brave, insipid

   (A) intrepid

   (B) fatuous

   (C) patent

   (D) surreptitious

Level C Vocabulary   www.testprofessors.com

17) Anomalous

   (A) manifest

   (B) quixotic

   (C) recondite

   (D) stouthearted

18) Perspicacious

   (A) calumnious

   (B) trenchant

   (C) flummoxed

   (D) intrepid

19) Excoriate

   (A) extol

   (B) vindicate

   (C) gainsay

   (D) reprobate   scold

20) Panegyric

   (A) encomium

   (B) expatiation

   (C) reiteration

   (D) insouciance

Answer Keys

Answer Keys

Answer Keys

Rapid Review 1

1) C
2) D
3) B
4) A
5) D
6) B
7) D
8) A

Rapid Review 2

1) D
2) B
3) C
4) B
5) D
6) A
7) D
8) B

Rapid Review 3

1) C
2) B
3) A
4) D
5) B
6) D
7) B
8) D

Answer Keys

Level A Review

1) C
2) D
3) A
4) B
5) D
6) C
7) B
8) C
9) D
10) A
11) A
12) D
13) D
14) B
15) D
16) C
17) D
18) D
19) B
20) C

Rapid Review 5

1) C
2) B
3) C
4) C
5) C
6) B
7) A
8) B

Answer Keys

Rapid Review 6

1) D
2) B
3) A
4) C
5) D
6) A
7) C
8) B

Rapid Review 7

1) B
2) D
3) C
4) A
5) B
6) C
7) B
8) B

Level B Review

1) C
2) B
3) C
4) C
5) C
6) A
7) C
8) B
9) C
10) D
11) B
12) C
13) C
14) D
15) B

Answer Keys

16) C
17) D
18) B
19) B
20) C

Rapid Review 9

1) B
2) B
3) D
4) B
5) C
6) B
7) A
8) C

Rapid Review 10

1) C
2) B
3) D
4) C
5) B
6) B
7) D
8) C

Rapid Review 11

1) C
2) A
3) C
4) C
5) B
6) A
7) B
8) A

Answer Keys

Level C Review

1) B
2) D
3) B
4) D
5) B
6) A
7) B
8) C
9) D
10) C
11) C
12) C
13) C
14) C
15) A
16) B
17) B
18) B
19) D
20) A

QUICK LISTS

To Explain

clarify   delineate   elucidate

demystify   expound

expatiate   exposit   lucubrate

To Argue For

affirm   contend   justify

advocate   corroborate   substantiate

aver   avow   vindicate

To Argue Against

dispel   dispute   rebut   refute

confute   debunk   dissent

controvert   gainsay   repugn

To Emphasize

stress   underscore

accentuate   punctuate

iterate   reiterate

Confused

bedeviled	dumbfounded	quizzical	
befuddled	bemused	confounded	vexed
addled	discombobulated	flummoxed	nonplussed

Mocking

spoof   taunt

jeer   scoff

deride   lampoon

Doubtful / Questioning

cynical   evaluative

appraising   incredulous

dubious   dubitable

Indifferent / Lazy

dispirited	idle	slothful	
apathetic	lackadaisical	languorous	nonchalant
indolent	insouciant	otiose	

Passionate

zeal	zest	
fervent	fervid	perfervid
ardent	avid	torrid

Praise

eulogy	exalt	hail	kudos
accolade	approbation	herald	paean
adulate	éclat	encomium	extol
plaudit			

Criticize / Scold

chasten	chastise	rebuke	reprove
berate	castigate	chide	animadversion
excoriate	remonstrate	reprobate	upbraid

Dislike / Hate

abominate	contempt	loathe
abhor	antipathy	disdain
animus	enmity	execrate

Flatter

bootlick	fawn	kowtow	
blandish	obsequious	sycophant	
inveigle	toady	truckle	wheedle

Insult

affront	deride	slight	
aspersion	besmirch	disparage	
calumny	contumely	obloquy	traduce

Smart

astute	canny	keen
erudite	sagacious	sage
perspicacious	sapient	trenchant

Stupid

dolt	dullard	obtuse
dupe	inane	vapid
fatuous	insipid	vacuous

Brave

dauntless gallant valorous

audacious lionhearted stalwart

intrepid mettlesome stout stouthearted

Different / Odd

divergent heterogeneous peculiar

aberrant disparate

anomalous quixotic singular

Widespread / Obvious

blatant conspicuous

egregious overt pervasive

manifest patent

Secret / Difficult to Understand

clandestine cryptic inscrutable

abstruse esoteric furtive

arcane recondite sub-rosa surreptitious

OTHER TITLES FROM FUSION PRESS

SAT Practice Test (Kindle Edition)

5 SAT Math Practice Tests

5 SAT Critical Reading Practice Tests

5 SAT Writing Practice Tests

10 SAT Vocabulary Practice Tests

5 Fantastically Hard SAT Math Practice Tests

5 Fantastically Hard SAT Critical Reading Practice Tests

5 Fantastically Hard SAT Writing Practice Tests

10 Fantastically Hard SAT Vocabulary Practice Tests

5 PSAT Math Practice Tests

5 PSAT Writing Practice Tests

10 PSAT Vocabulary Practice Tests

5 Fantastically Hard PSAT Math Practice Tests

5 Fantastically Hard PSAT Critical Reading Practice Tests

5 Fantastically Hard PSAT Writing Practice Tests

10 Fantastically Hard PSAT Vocabulary Practice Tests

Score-Raising Vocabulary Builder for ACT and SAT (Level 1)

Score-Raising Vocabulary Builder for ACT and SAT (Level 2)

Score-Raising Vocabulary Builder for ACT and SAT (Level 4)

Score-Raising Vocabulary Builder for GRE and GMAT (Level 2)

Score-Raising Vocabulary Builder for GRE and GMAT (Level 3)

Score-Raising Vocabulary Builder for GRE and GMAT (Level 4)

CPSIA information can be obtained at www.ICGtesting.com
Printed in the USA
LVOW01s1638270913

354474LV00012B/534/P